Waffle Cookbook

Delicious Waffle Recipes Made Easy

www.grizzlypublishing.com

Table of Contents

Introduction

First and foremost, I want to give you a massive thank you for purchasing my book, 'Waffle Cookbook: Delicious Waffle Recipes Made Easy.'

I can only assume that your first thought when seeing this book is 'why in the world would someone write an entire cookbook on waffles?'

After which you obviously answered your own question with the stark realization that 1) waffles are arguably the tastiest food on the planet, 2) you know next to nothing about the amazing waffle recipes that exist in the big wide world that you live in, and 3) you genuinely need this amazing book in your life.

Or something like that?

Anyhow, even if it didn't quite play out *exactly* in that manner, I am sure you would agree that waffles are a seriously delightful food.

Otherwise we wouldn't be having this conversation in the first place.

Seriously, anyone who has ever gotten the opportunity to take a bite out of the sweet, crisp, and mouthwatering meal that is a waffle, would understand the importance of this food. A historical American treat, waffles have long been integrated into our culture as the perfect breakfast meal that can be eaten savory or sweet.

But over the last few years waffles have seen a real resurgence around the globe. They have becoming increasingly popular as a versatile food that can be served throughout the day in a variety of settings, commonly as a decadent desert, a sweet and delicious breakfast, or even a healthy savory lunch.

And when I say versatile, I'm not simply talking about different toppings.

Waffles themselves have been changed, altered, and experimented with, to achieve some of the most incredible meals that you could imagine. Have you ever heard of red velvet waffles? Or carrot cake waffles?

What about pumpkin waffles? Mac and cheese waffles?

Waffle breakfast tacos?

Sausage waffles?

Well, you get the picture.

Waffles have become so much more than just a plain pastry breakfast (not that there is anything wrong with this sort of thing). Over the last few years they have evolved into a cuisine entirely unto themselves, being used for breakfast, lunch, dinner, and desert, in a variety of different ways, shapes and forms.

And you are about to uncover them all.

This cookbook contains an unbelievable number of waffle recipes that are suitable for literally every occasion. From sweet to savory, from pumpkin to potato, and from sausage to apple, this book has them all.

And I can assure you that every single one will produce something that is crispy, tasty, and perfect – and above all, I can also promise that they will be easy to prepare.

Each recipe is full to the brim with flavor, yet simple and easy to understand, making this book absolutely perfect for the novice cook and advanced chef alike.

So, what are you waiting for? Bring the batter out and let's start making waffles!

Almond Butter Waffles

Yields: 6

Ingredients

- 1 ¼ cup oatmeal flour (gluten-free)
- 4 tsp. of baking powder
- ½ tsp salt
- 2 tbsp organic almond butter
- 1 2/3 cup almond milk
- 2 egg whites
- ½ cup dark chocolate chips

Method

1. Preheat your waffle maker to medium heat setting.

2. Using a large bowl, mix all the dry ingredients together. In a separate medium bowl, pour in the wet ingredients and mix thoroughly.

3. Beat the eggs in a small bowl until they become foamy.

4. Pour the wet ingredients over the dry ingredients and thoroughly mix everything together. Fold in the egg whites into your batter.

5. Add chocolate chips then mix.

6. Grease your iron with cooking spray and pour batter onto the waffle maker. Add chocolate chips if desired.

7. Cook waffles until golden brown.

8. Add toppings of your choice then serve.

Apple Cinnamon Waffles

Yields: 6

Ingredients

- 2 cups all-purpose flour
- 3 Tablespoons sugar
- 2 teaspoons baking powder
- 1/2 teaspoon salt
- 2 large eggs - separated
- 1 and 1/4 cups milk
- 1/3 cup vegetable oil
- 1 apple - finely sliced
- 2 teaspoons cinnamon

Method

1. Sift sugar, flour, baking powder, and salt together. Set aside.

2. Beat egg whites in a small bowl until stiff then set aside.

3. Beat egg yolks well in a separate medium bowl. Stir in milk.

4. Pour sifted dry ingredients onto egg yolks and mix until moist.

5. Add vegetable oil.

6. Fold in egg whites and pour the cinnamon in the mixture. Stir.

7. Add apples then blend lightly into the mixture.

8. Bake in preheated waffle iron for 4 -5 minutes, until golden brown.

Apple Waffles

Yields: 6

Ingredients

- 2 cups milk
- 1 teaspoon cinnamon
- 2 large eggs
- 2 cups pancake mix
- 1/3 cup melted butter or margarine
- 1 cup finely chopped apple

Method

1. In a medium-sized bowl, mix eggs, milk, melted butter, and pancake mix. Beat with mixer until the batter is smooth.

2. Stir in apples.

3. Cook in a well-greased and heated iron until crisp and golden brown.

4. Serve warm and enjoy.

Bacon Cheddar Waffles

Yields: 4

Ingredients

- 1 large egg

- 1 cup milk

- 1 cup sour cream

- 1 Tablespoon butter or margarine - melted

- 2 cups Bisquick baking mix

- 6 bacon strips - cooked and crumbled

- 1 cup shredded Cheddar cheese

Method

1. In a medium bowl, beat the egg.

2. Add the milk, sour cream and melted butter. Add the baking mix and mix well.

3. Fold in the cooked and crumbled bacon strips and the Cheddar cheese.

4. Spoon batter onto a prepared, hot waffle iron. Close waffle iron and cook until golden brown, according to

the waffle maker's instructions.

5. Serve with maple syrup or your favorite fruit-flavored syrup.

Banana Bread Waffles

Yields: 6

Ingredients

- Cooking spray
- 2 c. all-purpose flour
- 1 tsp. baking soda
- 1/2 tsp. kosher salt
- 1/2 c. (1 stick) melted butter
- 1 c. sugar
- 1 large egg
- 1 large egg yolk
- 1/4 c. sour cream
- 1 tsp. of pure vanilla extract
- 3 ripe bananas, mashed with a fork
- 1 c. semisweet chocolate chips
- Maple syrup

Method

1. Preheat waffle maker then grease with cooking spray.
2. Using a large bowl, combine baking soda, flour and salt then whisk together.
3. Using a large separate bowl, mix and stir melted butter, egg, egg yolk, sour cream, sugar, and vanilla. Add the mashed bananas and stir until fully mixed.

Slowly pour dry ingredients over wet ingredients until combined. Add chocolate chips.

4. Pour batter onto waffle maker. Cook until both sides are golden. Put waffle on a plate. Repeat process for the remaining batter.

5. Drizzle maple syrup over warm waffles and serve.

Banana Cream Waffles

Yields: 6

Ingredients

- 2 cups flour
- 3 teaspoons baking powder
- 1 teaspoon salt
- 2 eggs
- 2 cups milk
- 1/3 cup vegetable oil
- 2 1/2 teaspoons banana cream baking flavoring

Method

1. Mix salt, flour, and baking powder in a medium-sized bowl.

2. Set aside.

3. Using another bowl, beat the eggs. Pour in the vegetable oil, milk, and banana cream flavoring. Stir until fully combined.

4. Add in the flour mixture and stir.

5. Heat the waffle iron and cook until golden brown.

Best Waffle Recipe

Yields: 5

Ingredients

- 1 and 3/4 cups flour
- 2 teaspoons baking powder
- 1 Tablespoon sugar
- 1/2 teaspoon salt
- 3 beaten egg yolks
- 1 and 3/4 cups milk
- 1/2 cup vegetable oil
- 3 egg whites - beaten stiffly

Method

1. Combine all the dry ingredients.
2. Stir the milk and the egg yolks together then pour into the dry ingredients.
3. Stir in oil and mix.
4. Carefully fold in beaten egg whites (don't over mix).

5. Cook according to your waffle maker's instructions.

6. Serve and enjoy.

Blueberry Waffles

Yields: 6-8

Ingredients

- 1 cup fresh or frozen blueberries
- 1 and 1/3 cups milk
- 2 large eggs - separated
- 1 teaspoon vanilla
- 2 cups all-purpose flour
- 2 Tablespoons sugar
- 2 teaspoons baking powder
- 2 pinches of salt
- 3/4 teaspoon cinnamon
- 1/3 cup butter - melted and cooled

Method

1. Separate egg whites and yolks.

2. Beat the yolks and milk together in a medium-sized bowl. Stir in the vanilla.

3. Using a separate bowl, sift the flour and stir in the sugar, baking powder, cinnamon, and salt. Pour in the milk and yolk mixture then whisk until smooth. Stir

in the melted butter.

4. Beat the egg whites until stiff peaks form. Fold egg whites into the batter.

5. Carefully fold the blueberries into the batter 1/3 cup at a time.

6. Heat the waffle iron and grease with a cooking spray. Cook until golden brown.

7. Serve warm and enjoy.

Bread and Butter Waffles

Yields: 4

Ingredients

- butter
- 2 eggs
- 1 cup milk
- 1 teaspoon sugar
- 1 dash salt
- 6 to 8 slices of bread

Method

1. Spread butter on both sides of bread.
2. Lightly beat the eggs. Add sugar, milk, and salt and blend thoroughly.
3. Dip the bread in the mixture.
4. Cook on a moderately hot waffle iron.
5. Serve with syrup.

Buttermilk Belgian Waffles

Yields: 3

Ingredients

- 4 medium eggs
- 1 packet of dry yeast
- 2 and 1/2 cup of flour
- 2 cups of lukewarm buttermilk
- 1/2 cup of melted butter
- 1 Tablespoon of sugar
- 1 teaspoon of vanilla
- 1/2 teaspoon of salt

Method

1. Sift together the flour, salt, and sugar in a bowl then set aside.

2. Using a second bowl, dissolve one packet of yeast in lukewarm buttermilk.

3. Separate the 4 eggs and keep the whites in a separate bowl. Beat the yolks then mix it with the buttermilk and yeast mixture then add the vanilla.

4. Pour the flour mixture to the buttermilk and egg yolk mixture then stir. Stir in the melted butter.

5. Beat the egg whites until they are stiff and peaked, then fold them into the batter. Let the batter sit for 20 to 45 minutes.

6. Cook in a well-greased and heated iron until crisp and golden brown.

7. Serve warm and enjoy.

Buttermilk Waffles

Yields: 20

Ingredients

- 1 and 1/2 cups all-purpose flour
- 1 teaspoon double-acting baking powder
- 1 teaspoon baking soda
- 1/2 teaspoon salt
- 2 cups buttermilk
- 1/3 cup canola oil
- 2 eggs - beaten
- 1/2 teaspoon vanilla (optional)

Method

1. Preheat your waffle iron.

2. Mix together the baking powder, flour, salt, and baking soda.

3. In a second bowl, mix the oil, eggs, buttermilk, and optional vanilla.

4. Pour wet ingredients over dry ingredients and whisk until mixed. Don't over mix.
5. Cook the waffles in a well-greased and heated waffle maker.

6. Serve and enjoy.

Butterscotch Waffles

Yields: 4

Ingredients

- 3/4 cup + 1 Tablespoon all-purpose flour
- 1/4 cup cornstarch
- 1 Tablespoon sugar
- 1/2 teaspoon salt
- 1/2 teaspoon baking powder
- 1/4 teaspoon baking soda
- 1 cup buttermilk or regular milk
- 6 tbs. of canola or vegetable oil (or melted butter)
- 1 large egg - separated
- 1/2 teaspoon vanilla extract
- 1/2 cup butterscotch chips

Method

1. Preheat waffle iron to medium-high.

2. Mix together the flour, sugar, cornstarch, salt, baking powder and soda in a large bowl. Using a separate medium bowl, stir the milk, egg yolk, oil and vanilla together until fully combined.

3. Beat the egg whites in another bowl until peaks form.

4. Pour in wet ingredients and butterscotch chips over the dry ingredients then stir until combined and moist. Gently fold in the egg white. The batter must be a little lumpy.

5. Pour in the batter onto your waffle iron. Cook until golden brown.

6. Serve with your favorite topping.

Carrot Cake Waffles (w/Maple Cream Cheese Drizzle)

Yields: 4-6

Ingredients

FOR THE MAPLE CREAM CHEESE GLAZE

- 4 oz. whipped cream cheese, softened
- 1/4 c. maple syrup

FOR THE WAFFLES

- 3/4 c. all-purpose flour
- 1/2 c. whole-wheat flour
- 1/2 c. cornstarch
- 3 tsp. baking powder
- 1 tsp. cinnamon
- 1/4 tsp. nutmeg
- 1/2 tsp. ground ginger
- 1/4 tsp. allspice
- 1/2 tsp. kosher salt
- 1 tbsp. brown sugar
- 2 large eggs
- 1/3 c. shredded coconut
- 1/3 c. vegetable oil
- 1 1/4 c. milk

- 1 c. carrot purée (cook the carrots until soft then purée using a food processor or blender)
- Melted butter, for waffle iron

Method

1. Make the glaze by whisking cream cheese and maple syrup together until smooth. Set aside.

2. Make the batter by whisking all waffle ingredients together in a large mixing bowl until fully combined.

3. Allow batter to rest for 15 to 20 minutes.

4. Heat up waffle maker, then grease with butter or cooking spray.

5. Pour 1/2 cup batter into the iron and cook until golden brown.

6. Repeat with the remaining batter. Drizzle with the glaze and serve.

Cereal Waffles

Yields: 6

Ingredients

- 1 cup all-purpose flour
- 2 tsp. baking powder
- 4 tbs. melted shortening
- 1/2 cup chopped raisins
- 1 cup breakfast cereal*
- 1 tsp. salt
- 1 cup milk
- 1 egg (beaten)
- 1 tbs. sugar

Method

1. Sift together flour, sugar, salt, and baking powder. Add the cereal and raisins then stir.
2. Using another bowl, whisk together the egg, shortening, and mix.
3. Combine the liquid and dry ingredients then stir until fully mixed and moistened.
4. Cook in the waffle iron until golden brown.
5. Serve with maple syrup.

Note:

- You can use other cereals as well (without mallows).

Chicken & Waffle Sandwich

Yields: 4

Ingredients

FOR THE WAFFLES

- 3 large eggs (separate whites from yolks)
- 1/2 c. all-purpose flour
- 1/2 c. baking soda
- 1 c. milk
- 2 tbsp. honey
- 4 tbsp. butter, melted
- 2 boxes cornbread mix

FOR THE FRIED CHICKEN

- 1 c. buttermilk
- 1 tbsp. Hot sauce
- 1 lb. chicken cutlets, sliced in half
- 1 1/2 c. all-purpose flour
- 2 tsp. garlic powder
- 1 tsp. paprika
- kosher salt
- Freshly ground black pepper
- Vegetable oil, for frying

Method

1. Preheat the waffle iron.

2. Whisk the egg whites to soft peaks and then set aside.

3. Whisk together all other waffle ingredients and fold in the egg whites.

4. Pour batter onto hot iron and cook until golden brown.

5. Fry the chicken: Using a bowl, marinate the chicken in buttermilk and add a dash of hot sauce.

6. Using a separate bowl, combine flour with garlic powder and paprika, then season with salt and pepper. Dredge the chicken in the flour.

7. Add 1 inch of oil in a cast-iron pan over medium-high heat and fry the chicken cutlets. Move to a paper towel to drain once golden brown and cooked.

8. Make the syrup in a small saucepan by adding bourbon and maple syrup.

9. Heat on medium-high for about 5 minutes to burn off alcohol and reduce liquid.

10. Remove from heat and whisk in butter. Allow to cool.

11. Put a piece of fried chicken between two waffles and drizzle with bourbon sauce.

12. Serve and enjoy.

Chocolate Brownie Waffles

Yields: 5

Ingredients

- 1/4 cup semi-sweet chocolate chips
- 3 tbs. unsweetened cocoa
- 1/3 cup chopped walnuts
- 1 3/4 cups pancake mix
- 3 tbs. sugar
- 1 large egg
- 1/4 cup vegetable oil
- 1 and 1/3 cups water

Method

1. Preheat waffle maker to its medium setting.

2. Using a medium-sized bowl, sift together the pancake, chocolate chips, walnuts, cocoa, and sugar.

3. Beat the egg in a separate bowl and stir in the water and oil.

4. Add wet ingredients over dry ingredients and mix with a whisk until large lumps disappear. Allow the batter to rest for 5 minutes.

5. Grease the waffle iron with butter or a cooking spray then pour desired amount of batter. Cook until golden brown then serve.

Chocolate Chip Waffles

Yields: 7-8

Ingredients

- 1 ½ cups of white whole-wheat flour
- ½ cup all-purpose flour
- 2 tbsp. cornstarch
- 1 tsp. baking powder
- ½ tsp. baking soda
- ½ tsp. salt
- 2 large eggs
- 1 ½ cups of buttermilk
- ½ cup milk
- 1 tbsp. pure maple syrup
- 1 ½ tsp. vanilla extract
- 3 tbsp. melted and slightly cooled butter
- ½ cup mini chocolate chips

Method

1. Whisk together white whole-wheat flour, all-purpose flour, baking powder, cornstarch, salt, and baking soda in a large bowl.

2. Using a separate medium bowl, whisk together milk, eggs, buttermilk, vanilla, and maple syrup. Whisk in the melted butter until fully combined.

3. Add wet ingredients into the dry ones then whisk until combined. Set aside.

4. Heat your waffle iron and grease it with a cooking spray.

5. Meanwhile, add mini chocolate chips into the waffle batter.

6. Cook waffles according to your manufacturer's instructions.

7. Serve warm and enjoy.

Chocolate Fudge Waffles

Yields: 6

Ingredients

- 2 ounces unsweetened baking chocolate
- 4 Tablespoons butter
- 3 large eggs
- 2/3 cup sugar
- 1 teaspoon vanilla extract
- 1 cup buttermilk
- 1 and 1/4 cups flour
- 1/2 teaspoon baking soda
- 1/2 teaspoon baking powder
- 1 pinch salt
- 3 ounces semisweet chocolate – chopped

Method

1. Preheat waffle iron.

2. In a microwave, melt the butter and chocolate together for 1 minute. Stir until smooth then allow it to cool.

3. Beat eggs, sugar, and vanilla together in a large bowl until fully mixed; stir in buttermilk. Pour in the reserved melted chocolate and mix thoroughly.

4. Stir in baking soda, flour, salt, and baking powder until smooth. Fold in the semisweet chocolate then add the batter onto the waffle maker and cook until golden brown.

5. Top with your favorite toppings and serve.

Chocolate Stout Waffle Sundae

Yields: 2-3

Ingredients

For The Sauce

- ½ cup stout
- 2 tbs. corn syrup
- 1 cup dark chocolate chips
- 3 tbs. butter

For the Waffles

- 2 tsp baking powder
- 1/4 cup cocoa powder
- 1/2 tsp salt
- 1/2 cup dark chocolate chips
- 1/3cup milk
- 2/3 cup stout
- 1/4 cup vegetable oil
- 1 tsp vanilla extract
- 2 eggs, divided
- 1/3 cup sugar
- Ice Cream for serving
- 1 cup flour

Method

1. Add 1/2 cup stout, butter, and corn syrup to a sauce pan. Cook in medium high heat until the butter has melted and the mixture has started boiling.

2. Turn the heat off and stir in 1 cup of chocolate chips until fully melted. Let it cool slightly before using.

3. Preheat the waffle maker.

4. Using a large bowl, add the baking powder, cocoa powder, flour, and salt, then stir.

5. Using a microwave safe bowl, add the milk and chocolate chips. Microwave for 20-30 seconds until melted. Add in the beer, vegetable oil, vanilla and only the yolks of the two eggs and then stir.

6. In a separate bowl, add the egg whites along with the sugar. Whip for about 5 minutes until soft peaks form.

7. Make a hole in the middle of the dry ingredients, pour in the chocolate milk mixture and stir until fully combined. Gently fold into the egg whites until thoroughly incorporated.

8. Cook in waffle and use butter or cooking spray if needed.

9. Top with ice cream and drizzle with chocolate sauce. Serve with a malty stout.

Chocolate waffles with peanut butter yogurt sauce

Yields: 2-3

Ingredients

- 1/2 cup almond flour
- 1/2 cup brown rice flour
- 1/2 cup gluten free baking flour
- 1/4 cup unsweetened cocoa powder
- 1 tablespoon cornstarch
- 1 teaspoon baking powder
- 1/2 teaspoon salt
- 2 eggs
- 3 tablespoons turbinado/raw sugar
- 1 teaspoon vanilla extract
- 2 tablespoons butter, melted
- 1 cup milk
- 1/4 cup dark chocolate chips

For the peanut butter sauce
- 1/4 cup plain Greek yogurt
- 2 tablespoons creamy natural peanut butter
- 1 tablespoon maple syrup
- 1-2 tablespoons milk

Method

1. Mix the flours, baking powder, cocoa powder, cornstarch, and salt in a large bowl.

2. Using a small bowl, whisk the eggs and sugar together.

3. Pour the butter, vanilla and milk then whisk until smooth.

4. Pour wet ingredients over the dry ingredients then whisk.

5. Add the chocolate chips.

6. Set aside for 15 minutes.

7. Preheat and grease your waffle maker.

8. Pour 3/4 cup of the batter into the iron and cook according to your waffle maker's directions.

9. Repeat the process for the remaining batter.

For the peanut butter sauce

1. Mix the peanut butter, yogurt, and maple syrup in a bowl until smooth.

2. Slowly add 1 tablespoon of milk and stir until you reach the desired consistency.

Cinnamon Belgian Waffles

Yields: 3

Ingredients

- 1 cup all-purpose flour
- 1 Tablespoon sugar
- 1 and 1/2 teaspoons baking powder
- 1/2 teaspoon baking soda
- 1/2 teaspoon ground cinnamon
- 1/4 teaspoon salt
- 1 cup buttermilk
- 2 large egg (separate yolks from whites)
- 1/4 cup butter - melted
- 1 teaspoon vanilla extract

Method

1. Preheat your waffle iron.

2. Mix the sugar, flour, baking powder, soda, salt, and cinnamon in a large mixing bowl.

3. In a separate bowl, mix the egg yolks, buttermilk, vanilla, and melted butter.

4. In a third bowl, beat the egg whites with an electric mixer until stiff peaks are forming.

5. Pour in wet ingredients to the dry ones and mix until evenly combined and moistened.

6. Carefully fold the egg whites into the mixture.

7. Cook in a well-greased waffle iron then serve warm.

Cinnamon Waffles

Yields: 6

Ingredients

- 2 eggs
- 3/4 cup milk
- 2 Tablespoons vegetable oil
- 1 cup flour
- 1 and 1/2 teaspoon baking powder
- 1 and 1/2 teaspoon sugar
- 1/2 teaspoon salt
- 1 teaspoon cinnamon

Method

1. Using a medium bowl, beat the eggs until it starts thickening. Add oil and milk.
2. Add dry ingredients then mix until smooth.

3. Cook the waffles in a well-greased and heated waffle maker.

4. Serve warm and enjoy.

Classic Waffle Batter

Yields: 4 Waffles

Ingredients

- 3 large eggs
- 1 1/2 c. whole milk
- 1 tsp. apple cider vinegar
- 1/2 c. canola oil
- 1 3/4 c. all-purpose flour
- 1/4 tsp. kosher salt
- 2 tsp. baking powder
- 1 tsp. baking soda
- Cooking spray, for waffle iron

Method

1. Preheat your waffle iron. Using a large mixing bowl, combine the eggs, milk, apple cider vinegar, and canola oil and then start whisking.

2. Using a separate bowl, whisk baking powder, salt, flour, and baking soda together. Then, pour dry ingredients into wet ones and start stirring.

3. Use the cooking spray to your heated waffle iron.

4. Pour the batter into the waffle iron until it is entirely covered.

5. Cook for about 3 minutes until it is golden.

6. Repeat the process with the remaining batter then serve the waffles when you're done.

Coconut Raspberry Waffles (w/ Coconut Whipped Cream)

Yields: 6

Ingredients

FOR THE WAFFLES

- 1 tablespoons granulated sugar
- 1 teaspoon baking powder
- 1/4 teaspoon salt
- 1 3/4 cup milk
- 1 teaspoon vanilla extract
- 2 large eggs
- 1/4 cup coconut oil, melted and cooled
- 1/2 cup shredded coconut
- 1 cup raspberries, fresh or frozen
- 1 3/4 cup White Whole Wheat Flour

FOR THE COCONUT WHIPPED CREAM

- 1 can full fat coconut milk, refrigerated overnight
- 1 tablespoon powdered sugar
- 1/2 teaspoon vanilla extract

Method

1. Using a large bowl, whisk flour, sugar, baking powder, and salt together. Then set aside.

2. In a separate medium bowl, whisk together milk, vanilla, eggs, and coconut oil. Pour the liquid ingredients into the dry ingredients and stir until thoroughly combined. Slowly stir in the coconut and raspberries.

3. Add the batter into a hot waffle iron and cook.

4. To make coconut whipped cream, scoop the top layer of white coconut milk into the bowl of stand mixer. Dispose the coconut water. Beat the coconut milk on high speed about 20 seconds using the whisk attachment until the mixture turns to liquid. Pour in the powdered sugar and vanilla then mix on high speed for 1-2 minutes, until it turns creamy.

5. Drizzle the waffle with coconut whipped cream and serve.

Corn Flake Waffles

Yields: 4

Ingredients

- 1 1/2 cups of sifted all-purpose flour
- 3 tablespoons white cornmeal
- 2 teaspoons sugar
- 2 cups finely crushed corn flakes
- 2 well beaten eggs
- 3 teaspoons baking powder
- 4 Tablespoons canola oil/melted shortening
- 2 and 1/2 cups milk

Method

1. In a large bowl, sift together the cornmeal, flour, salt, sugar, and baking powder.

2. Add corn flakes, oil/melted shortening, and eggs.

3. Add milk to make a thick batter.

4. Cook in a greased waffle iron.

5. Serve warm and enjoy.

Cornbread Waffles

Yields: 6 Waffles

Ingredients

- 1 c. buttermilk
- 1/2 c. butter, melted
- 6 tbsp. sugar
- 2 large eggs
- 1 c. all-purpose flour
- 1 1/2 c. yellow cornmeal
- 1 1/2 tsp. of baking powder
- 1 tsp. baking soda
- 1/4 tsp. kosher salt
- Cooking spray
- 1 tsp. honey
- 2 tbsp. softened butter, for serving

Method

1. Preheat your waffle iron and preheat the oven to 200° to keep your waffles warm.

2. Meanwhile, combine buttermilk, butter, sugar and eggs, and then whisk it together. Using a separate bowl, combine salt, cornmeal, flour, baking powder and soda. Combine wet mixture and dry ingredients then stir until moist.

3. Use cooking spray on your waffle iron. Then, pour about 1/4 cup of batter into the iron. Cook for 2 to 3 minutes per waffle until golden brown.

4. Remove cooked waffles then place on a baking sheet and keep warm in oven.

5. Repeat process with the remaining batter.

6. Mix softened butter with honey and drizzle the mixture over warm waffles.

Crispiest Waffle

Yields: 8

Ingredients

- 2 and 1/4 cups all-purpose flour
- 2 tbsp. sugar
- 1/2 teaspoon salt
- 1 stick butter (1/2 cup - melted then cooled)
- 2 cups warm whole milk (110 degrees)
- 2 teaspoons vanilla extract
- 2 large eggs – separated
- 1 teaspoon instant yeast (not active dry)

Method

The night before:

1. Stir the flour, yeast, sugar and salt together.
2. Stir melted butter into dry ingredients.
3. Stir in the vanilla and milk until fully combined.
4. Cover with plastic wrap and leave on the counter overnight.

In the morning:

5. The batter should look bubbly. Heat your waffle maker

6. Add egg yolks to the batter then whip the egg whites to stiff peaks then fold into the batter carefully.

7. The batter will rise a bit more than usual, so test out a waffle before starting.

Dark Chocolate Waffles

Yields: 6

Ingredients

- 2 cups all-purpose flour
- ½ cup unsweetened cocoa powder
- ¼ cup brown sugar
- 2 teaspoons baking powder
- 1 teaspoon baking soda
- 1 teaspoon kosher salt
- 3 large eggs, separated
- 2 cups buttermilk
- ½ cup olive oil
- 1 teaspoon vanilla extract
- 6 oz. bittersweet finely chopped chocolate (at least 70% cacao)
- Nonstick vegetable oil spray
- Unsalted butter, maple syrup and peanut butter – for serving

Method

1. Preheat your oven to 250°. Whisk cocoa powder, flour, baking powder, brown sugar, salt, and baking soda in a large bowl.

2. Make a hole in the center and add buttermilk, egg yolks, vanilla, and oil.

3. Blend, then slowly add dry ingredients and mix until combined.

4. In a small bowl, beat egg whites until soft peaks form.

5. Working in two batches, fold egg whites into the batter until combined. Fold in the chocolate.

6. Cook the batter in a well-greased waffle iron.

7. Serve with butter and syrup.

Egg-Free Waffles

Yields: 4

Ingredients

- 1 cup all-purpose flour
- 1/4 cup wheat flour
- 2 teaspoons baking powder
- 2 Tablespoons sugar
- 3 Tablespoons canola oil
- 1 1/4 cup of cool water
- dash of salt

Method

1. In a medium bowl, sift dry ingredients together.

2. Make a well-like hole in the middle of the mixture and pour in water and oil. Stir until wet.

3. Cook in a well-greased waffle iron and serve with butter and syrup.

Eggnog Waffles

Yields: 4

Ingredients

- 2 cups all-purpose flour
- 2 cups eggnog
- 1 cup finely chopped walnuts or pecans
- 2 large beaten eggs
- 6 Tablespoons vegetable oil
- 2 teaspoons baking powder
- 1 teaspoon baking soda
- 1/2 teaspoon salt

Method

1. Using a large bowl, sift the flour, baking soda, baking powder, and salt.

2. In a second bowl, combine the eggs, eggnog, and oil until fully mixed.

3. Add wet ingredients to the dry ingredients.

4. Mix until smooth then fold in the nuts.

5. Cook waffles in a well-greased heated waffle iron.

6. Serve and enjoy.

Note: The nuts are optional

Gingerbread Waffles

Yields: 3

Ingredients

- 3 large eggs
- 1/4 cup sugar
- 1/2 cup molasses
- 1 cup buttermilk
- 1 and 1/2 cups all-purpose flour
- 1 teaspoon ground ginger
- 1/2 teaspoon ground cinnamon
- 1/2 teaspoon ground cloves
- 1/2 teaspoon salt
- 1 teaspoon baking soda
- 1 teaspoon baking powder
- 6 Tablespoon (3/4 stick) melted butter

Method

1. Preheat waffle iron to medium setting.

2. Beat the eggs until light and foamy in a small bowl. Add molasses, sugar, and buttermilk, and then beat.

3. Using a large bowl, sift together the ginger, flour, cloves, cinnamon, salt, baking powder and baking soda.

4. Add to the batter then stir until smooth. Add the butter and mix.

5. Cook in a well-greased waffle iron for about 4 to 5 minutes.

6. Serve warm and enjoy.

Grape-Nuts Waffles

Yields: 4

Ingredients

- 1 1/2 cups sifted flour
- 2 teaspoons Calumet Baking Powder
- 1/2 teaspoon salt
- 1 Tablespoon sugar
- 1/2 cup Grape-Nuts
- 2 well beaten egg yolks
- 1 and 1/2 cups milk
- 2 Tablespoons melted butter
- 2 egg whites - stiffly beaten
- 1/2 cups additional Grape-Nuts

Method

1. Sift flour, baking powder, sugar, and salt. Add 1/2 cup of Grape-Nuts and mix thoroughly.

2. Mix egg yolks, butter, and milk then add to the flour mixture. Beat until smooth. Fold in egg whites.

3. Cook in a hot waffle iron and add about 2 Tablespoons of Grape-Nuts to each waffle before closing the iron.

4. Serve warm and enjoy.

Greek Yogurt Waffles

Yields: 4

Ingredients

- 2 eggs
- 1 3/4 cup milk
- 1/2 cup plain Greek yogurt
- 1 tbsp. sugar or maple syrup
- 2 cups flour
- 1 1/2 tablespoons baking powder
- 1/4 tsp. salt

Method

1. Preheat your waffle iron.
2. Whisk the eggs, Greek yogurt, milk, and sugar all together in a medium bowl.

3. Add baking powder, salt, and flour then mix until ingredients are fully combined.

4. Grease the waffle iron and cook waffles according to manufacturer's instructions.

5. Serve with butter, berries, syrup, whipped cream, or powdered sugar.

Grilled Cheese Wafflewich Sliders (Vegan & Gluten Free)

Yields: 2

Ingredients

- 1 cup gluten free all purpose flour
- 1 tablespoon baking powder
- 1/2 cup club soda
- 1 tablespoon nutritional yeast
- pinch salt
- crispy lettuce leaves
- tomato slices
- cashew cheese sauce or dairy free slices
- 1 cup grated zucchini

Method

1. Using a mixing bowl, mix grated zucchini, baking powder, flour, club soda, nutritional yeast, and salt. Whip thoroughly until fully combined. Let the batter to rest for several minutes, and then whip again.

2. Scoop batter into middle of a non stick waffle maker using a 1/3 cup measure. Close and cook for about 3-4 minutes on one side then flip to cook the other side.

3. Cut each waffle into quarters.

4. Cut waffle quarter open to create two slices of "bread". Spoon cheese on one side of waffle. Add

tomato and lettuce on top of melted cheese then cover with another waffle slice.

Ham Waffles

Yields: 4

Ingredients

- 2 cups sifted flour
- 1 cup smoked Ham (uncooked and diced)
- 1 3/4 cups milk
- 2 well beaten egg yolks
- 2 stiffly beaten egg whites
- 1/3 cup melted butter
- 1 Tablespoon sugar
- 2 teaspoons baking powder
- 1/2 teaspoon salt
- 1/4 teaspoon baking soda

Method

1. Combine flour, baking powder, soda, sugar, and salt then sift together.

2. Using a separate bowl, mix the milk, egg yolks, and butter.

3. Pour the wet ingredients over the flour mixture and stir until smooth. Fold in the egg whites.

4. Cook on a hot waffle iron and add 1/4 cup of ham over the batter before closing the iron.

5. Serve warm and enjoy.

Lemon Waffles

Yields: 4

Ingredients

- 4 large eggs (separated)
- 1/4 cup sugar
- 1/2 teaspoon salt
- 1 cup milk
- 1 Tablespoon fresh lemon juice
- grated peel of 1 entire lemon
- 1/4 cup melted butter
- 1 and 1/4 cups flour
- 1/2 teaspoon baking powder

Method

1. Beat the egg yolks together with the salt and sugar in a medium bowl.

2. Blend in the lemon juice, milk, butter, and lemon peel then beat well.

3. Add the baking powder and flour.

4. Beat the egg whites until stiff and then fold into the batter.

5. Cook in a well-greased waffle iron until golden brown.

6. Serve with maple syrup and enjoy.

Liege Belgian Waffles

Yields: 4-5

Ingredients

- 1 C Belgian pearl sugar*
- 1 C melted butter
- 3 eggs
- 1 package yeast (2 tsp.)
- ⅓ C lukewarm water
- 1½ tbsp. granulated sugar
- ⅛ t salt
- 2 C flour

Method

1. Combine yeast, 1½ sugar and salt into lukewarm water. Wait until yeast is dissolved and sit for 15 minutes (it should be foamy). In the meantime, melt the butter.

2. Put flour in a large bowl. Create a hole in the middle and add in the yeast mixture. Whisk the eggs together and melted butter and add to the flour as well. Knead until you get a nice, even dough. Let it rest and rise until dough doubles.

3. Gently mix in the pearl sugar.

4. Let dough rest for another 15 minutes. Preheat Belgian waffle iron.

5. Place waffle dough into the waffle maker and bake for 3-5 minutes. Since the sugar will be mixed into

the dough later in the process, it will melt and caramelize and give you that special Liege waffle taste. Carefully remove waffles from the iron as the sugar can be hot and sticky. Allow the waffles to cool.

Notes

The batter must be thick as dough. It shouldn't pour at all. Press waffle iron down over the dough to flatten it out to bake. When waffles are cooked, prod it out of the waffle iron. They might be floppy when first baked. Let them cool on a cooling rack as they become crispy since the caramelized sugar needs to cool down to get hard.

Mac 'N Cheese Waffles

Yields: 10

Ingredients

- 2 tbsp. butter
- 1/4 c. milk
- 1 1/2 c. shredded Cheddar cheese (divided)
- 1 egg, beaten
- 1/3 c. bread crumbs
- Nonstick cooking spray, for the waffle iron
- 1 (6-8 oz) box macaroni and cheese

Method

1. Cook macaroni for about 7-8 minutes in a medium saucepan filled with boiling water and drain.

2. In the same pot, melt 2 tablespoons of butter over low heat. Add milk and cheese packet then whisk thoroughly.

3. Turn the heat off and return macaroni to pot. Add 1 cup of cheddar and stir until the cheese had melted and the macaroni is fully coated with the cheese sauce. Stir in bread crumbs and eggs until fully combined.

4. Meanwhile, preheat your waffle iron.

5. When hot enough, grease with cooking spray. Scoop ½ cup of the macaroni and cheese into the center of

the iron and add more cheese to the top. Close the iron and cook for about 5 minutes until golden brown. Carefully remove the waffle from the iron. Repeat process for the remaining Mac 'n cheese.

6. Serve and enjoy.

Maple Bacon Waffles

Yields: 8

Ingredients

- 8 slices of cooked and crumbled bacon
- 2 cups all-purpose flour
- 2 teaspoons baking powder
- 3/4 teaspoon salt
- 1 and 1/3 cups milk
- 2 large lightly beaten eggs
- 2 Tablespoons pure maple syrup
- 2 Tablespoons melted butter

Method

1. Preheat your waffle iron.

2. Mix together the baking powder, flour, and salt in a large bowl.

3. Using a separate bowl, beat together eggs, milk, butter, and syrup.

4. Add wet ingredients to the dry ones and mix until combined.

5. Pour batter onto your waffle maker and sprinkle each waffle with 1/8 of the bacon crumbles. Then, close

the iron and cook until golden brown.

6. Top the waffles with softened butter and maple syrup.

7. Serve and enjoy.

Maple Walnut Waffles

Yields: 4

Ingredients

- 2 cups all-purpose flour
- 1 and 1/2 cups buttermilk
- 1/2 cup pure maple syrup
- 1/2 cup chopped walnuts
- 1/3 cup vegetable shortening
- 2 large eggs - beaten
- 1 and 1/2 teaspoons baking powder
- 1/2 teaspoon baking soda
- 1/4 teaspoon salt

Method

1. Preheat your waffle iron.

2. In a large bowl, combine the buttermilk, flour, shortening, maple syrup, eggs, baking soda, baking powder, and salt. Beat until the batter becomes light. Fold in walnuts.

3. Cook in a well-greased and heated iron until crisp and golden brown.

4. Serve warm and enjoy.

Mozzarella Stick Waffles

Yields: 8

Ingredients

- 1 c. all-purpose flour
- 2 large eggs, lightly beaten
- 2 tbsp. milk (or water)
- 1 c. Italian bread crumbs
- kosher salt
- 16 mozzarella sticks
- Chopped parsley
- Warm Marinara for serving

Method

1. Preheat waffle iron to medium heat.

2. Set up a dredging station then add flour to a shallow bowl.

3. Using another separate shallow bowl, whisk eggs and milk together. In a third shallow bowl, season your bread crumbs with salt.

4. Add mozzarella sticks in flour, add in egg mixture until evenly coated, then toss in the bread crumbs.

5. Grease waffle iron with nonstick cooking spray. Place coated mozzarella sticks side by side in the hot waffle

iron. Cover and cook for about 4 minutes until golden brown.

6. Carefully remove the waffles then slice waffles into thin strips. Top with parsley and serve with marinara sauce.

Multi-Grain Waffles

Yields: 6

Ingredients

- 2 cups buttermilk or regular milk
- 1/2 cup quick or old-fashioned rolled oats
- 2 large lightly beaten eggs
- 1/4 cup packed brown sugar
- 2 Tablespoon canola oil
- 2 teaspoons vanilla extract
- 2/3 cup whole-wheat flour
- 2/3 cup all-purpose flour
- 1/4 cup wheat germ - pan-toasted until it smells nutty
- 1 and 1/2 teaspoons baking powder
- 1/2 teaspoon baking soda
- 1 teaspoon ground cinnamon
- 1/4 teaspoon salt

Method

1. Combine together the oats and milk. Set aside for 15 minutes.

2. Add the eggs, oil, brown sugar, and vanilla then mix well

3. Using a separate bowl, mix the wheat germ, flours, baking soda, cinnamon, salt, and baking powder.

4. Pour the wet ingredients over the dry ones then stir until evenly combined. The batter must be a bit lumpy.

5. Cook according to your waffle maker's instructions or until it is crisp and golden brown.

6. Serve and enjoy.

Omelet Waffles

Yields: 1

Ingredients

- kosher salt
- Freshly ground black pepper
- 2 tbsp. chopped ham
- 1/4 c. shredded Cheddar
- 2 tsp. Freshly Chopped Parsley
- 3 large eggs

Method

1. Beat eggs in a large bowl.

2. Season with salt and pepper, and then add in ham, cheddar, and parsley.

3. Grease waffle iron with cooking spray, and then pour in the egg mixture.

4. Cook on low for about 4 to 5 minutes until fluffy and lightly golden

5. Serve immediately.

Oreo Cheesecake Waffles

Yields: 1

Ingredients

FOR THE WAFFLES:

- 1/2 c. sugar
- 1 tbsp. baking powder
- 2 tbsp. cocoa powder
- 1 tsp. salt
- 2 eggs
- 1 1/2 c. milk
- 8 tbsp. butter, melted
- 20 Oreo cookies, crushed

FOR THE CHEESECAKE CREAM:

- 8 oz. softened cream cheese
- 1 c. heavy cream
- 1/2 c. powdered sugar
- 8 Oreo cookies, roughly chopped
- Whipped cream for topping

Method

1. Preheat your waffle iron.

2. Mix sugar, flour, baking powder, cocoa powder and salt in a large bowl until fully mixed.

3. Add the milk, eggs, and melted butter then stir until fully combined. Fold in the crushed Oreos.

4. Grease your waffle iron and pour about 1/3 cup of batter onto the waffle maker and cook according to manufacturer's instructions.

5. Repeat process with remaining batter then set waffles aside.

6. Beat softened cream cheese in a separate medium bowl until smooth. Add in the heavy cream and powdered sugar then beat until soft peaks form.

7. Top each waffle with the cheesecake filling then repeat with other waffles. Add chopped Oreos and whipped cream in each waffle.

8. Serve and enjoy.

Overnight Waffle Batter

Yields: 8

Ingredients

- 2 teaspoons sugar
- 1/2 cup warm water (preferably 110 degrees)
- 1 package of active dry yeast
- 2 large eggs
- 2 cups milk
- 1/2 cup melted butter or canola oil
- 1 teaspoon vanilla
- 2 cups all-purpose flour
- 1 teaspoon salt
- 1/2 teaspoon cinnamon
- 1/4 teaspoon grated nutmeg

Method

1. Dissolve the sugar in warm water. Stir in the yeast and leave for 5 minutes until foam is starting to show.

2. Lightly beat the eggs in a medium bowl then add the melted butter, vanilla, and milk. Whisk until fully combined.

3. Combine together the nutmeg, cinnamon, flour, and salt in a large bowl. Add the milk mixture and the yeast mixture then stir until fully combined.

4. Cover with a plastic wrap and refrigerate overnight.

5. Remove the batter from the refrigerator in the morning and stir. Set aside for 15 minutes.

6. Cook the waffles according to your waffle maker's instructions or until they are crisp and golden brown. Serve.

Peach Waffles

Yields: 6

Ingredients

- 1/3 cup butter
- 1/2 cup sugar
- 2 large eggs
- 2 cups all-purpose flour
- 2 teaspoons baking powder
- 1/2 teaspoon salt
- 1 cup milk
- 1 and 1/2 cup sliced peaches
- 1/2 teaspoon vanilla
- 1/2 teaspoon lemon juice

Method

1. Cream the sugar and butter together in a large bowl

2. Add the eggs and beat until fully mixed.

3. Sift the flour with the salt and baking powder in a separate bowl.

4. Pour the flour mixture over the egg mixture along with the lemon juice, milk, and vanilla.

5. Mix thoroughly and fold in the peach pieces.

6. Cook in a well-greased waffle iron.

7. Serve and enjoy.

Peanut Butter Waffles

Yields: 8

Ingredients

- 1 cup whole wheat flour
- 1/4 cup milk powder (1/3 cup instant)
- 1/2 teaspoon salt
- 2 teaspoons baking powder
- 2 large eggs - beaten
- 1/4 cup honey
- 1/2 teaspoon vanilla
- 1/2 cup peanut butter
- 1 and 1/4 cups water (or milk)

Method

1. In a large mixing bowl, stir together the milk powder, flour, baking powder, and salt.

2. In a second bowl, beat the eggs, vanilla, honey, and peanut butter. Then mix in the water.

3. Add liquid mixture to the dry ingredients and stir until smooth.

4. Cook on a hot and well-greased waffle iron until crisp and golden brown.

5. Serve and enjoy.

Pecan Waffles (Egg-Free)

Yields: 4

Ingredients

- 3 1/2 Tablespoons of finely ground golden flax seed
- 12 Tablespoons water
- 1 and 1/2 cups plain soy milk
- 1 Tablespoon vinegar
- 1 and 1/2 cups unbleached self-rising flour
- 3 Tablespoons maple syrup
- 3 Tablespoons canola oil
- 3/4 cup finely chopped pecans

Method

1. Beat the finely ground flax seed with water until it has a beaten-egg-like consistency.

2. Combine vinegar with soy milk and let it sit for a few minutes.

3. Add flour a half cup at a time to the flax seed mixture, alternating with 1/2 cup of the curdled soy milk, until all are evenly combined.

4. Mix in canola oil and maple syrup then add pecans.

5. Cook in a hot waffle maker until steam slows. Serve and enjoy.

Note: This recipe uses finely ground flaxseed and water as a substitute for eggs.

Perfect Belgian Waffles

Yields: 9 (7-inch round waffles)

Ingredients

- 3 cups warm milk
- 3 egg - separated
- 3/4 cup butter
- 2/3 cup sugar
- 2 teaspoons vanilla extract
- 1 and 1/2 teaspoons salt
- 4 cups all-purpose flour
- 1 1/4-ounce package active dry yeast

Method

1. Using a small bowl, dissolve the yeast in 1/4 cup of warm milk. Let it stand for 10 minutes until creamy.

2. Melt the butter in the microwave or in a sauce pan. Set aside until it's the same temperature as the milk.

3. In a separate large bowl, beat the egg yolks. Pour in 1/4 cup of warm milk and the melted butter then mix well. Add the yeast mixture, vanilla, sugar, and salt then stir. Stir in the flour alternately with the remaining milk.

4. Using a separate bowl, beat the egg whites until soft peaks form. Carefully fold the egg whites into the batter. Cover the bowl with a plastic wrap and let the batter rise for 1 hour.

5. Preheat your iron and cook according to your waffle iron's instructions.

Note:

For best results, the milk must be 110 degrees. You can make this recipe the night before and refrigerate the batter then use within 12 hours.

Pizza Waffles

Yields: 4

Ingredients

- Cooking spray
- 1 (16.3-oz.) can refrigerated biscuits
- 2 c. shredded mozzarella
- 1/4 c. pizza sauce
- 1 c. sliced mini pepperoni
- Freshly grated Parmesan, for garnish

Method

1. Preheat waffle iron and grease with cooking spray.

2. Roll out biscuits into flat patties using your hands or a rolling pin. Top half of biscuits with 1/2 cup of mozzarella and a tablespoon of pizza sauce.

3. Sprinkle with pepperoni. Top each with another biscuit and seal the edges.

4. Cook for about 3 minutes until waffles are golden.

5. Sprinkle with Parmesan.

6. Serve and enjoy.

Potato, Egg and Cheese Waffles

Yields: 2

Ingredients

- 1 1/3 cup of potatoes
- 1 egg
- 3 pieces of pre-cooked diced bacon
- 1/8 cup of shredded cheese (or more)
- Salt and pepper

Method

1. Preheat your waffle iron.

2. Combine egg, potatoes, cheese, bacon, and salt and pepper in a mixing bowl.

3. Heat the iron and grease it with a cooking spray. Pour the potato mixture into the waffle maker.

4. Cook waffles for about 5 minutes and/or until golden brown.

5. Serve warm and enjoy.

Pumpkin Waffles

Yields: 6

Ingredients

- 1 large egg – beaten
- 2 egg whites – beaten
- 4 Tablespoons brown sugar
- 1 cup evaporated skim milk
- 2 Tablespoons vegetable oil
- 1/2 cup canned pumpkin puree
- 2 teaspoons of vanilla
- 1 cup all-purpose flour
- 2 teaspoons baking powder
- 1/4 teaspoon salt
- 1 and 1/2 teaspoons cinnamon
- 1/2 teaspoon grated nutmeg
- 1/4 teaspoon ginger
- 1/4 teaspoon ground cloves
- 1/2 cup of apples - finely diced
- 1/4 cup of toasted walnuts

Method

1. Beat eggs, egg whites, milk, sugar, pumpkin, oil, and vanilla.

2. Combine dry ingredients.

3. Add the dry mixture to egg mixture until just combined (don't over-mix).

4. Fold in nuts and apples.

5. Pour in the batter onto your waffle maker and cook until light brown.

Rainbow Waffles

Yields: 2-3

Ingredients

- 4 c. Bisquick
- 2 c. milk
- 4 eggs
- 2 tbsp. granulated sugar
- 1 tsp. pure vanilla extract
- Orange, red, yellow, green, blue, purple food coloring
- Cooking spray, for waffle maker
- Whipped cream, for serving

Method

1. Using a large bowl, combine Bisquick, milk, sugar, vanilla, and eggs and whisk together.

2. Divide your batter into 6 medium-sized bowls then dye each bowl of batter using different rainbow colors. Using a Ziploc bag or a piping, transfer each colored batter into the bag.

3. Preheat your waffle iron. Beginning with purple, pipe a circle around the edge of the waffle iron. Quickly pipe a blue circle inside the purple one, and repeat the process with other colors. Close the iron and wait

until batter is cooked. Transfer cooked waffle on a plate and repeat the process for the remaining batter.

4. Create a rainbow by cutting the waffles in a half semi-circle.

5. Add whip cream then serve.

Red Velvet Waffles

Yields: 6

Ingredients

- 1 box red velvet cake mix
- 4 eggs
- 2 c. milk
- nonstick cooking spray
- 4 tbsp. cream cheese, softened
- 2 c. powdered sugar
- 1/4 c. whole milk
- 1/2 c. Mini chocolate chips, for garnish

Method

1. Preheat waffle iron on medium heat.

2. Using a large bowl, combine eggs, milk, and cake mix. Whisk until thoroughly mixed and smooth.

3. Using a separate medium bowl, mix powdered sugar, cream cheese, and milk. Stir until smooth. If you're opting for a thicker glaze, add more powdered sugar.

4. Grease waffle iron with a cooking spray. Pour batter into iron and cook for about 5-6 minutes.

5. Remove waffles from iron and drizzle with cream cheese glaze. Add mini chocolate chips then serve.

Sausage Waffles

Yields: 6

Ingredients

- 1/2 pound ground breakfast sausage
- 1 and 3/4 cups flour
- 2 tsp. of baking powder
- 1/2 tsp. salt
- 3 large eggs
- 1 and 3/4 cups milk
- 1/3 cup melted and room temp.

Method

1. Cook and crumble the breakfast sausage in a pan over medium heat. When cooked through, move to stacked paper towels to drain excess fat.

2. Using a large bowl, fully mix the flour, salt, and baking powder.

3. Using a separate bowl, beat the egg until foamy. Pour in the milk and melted butter then stir thoroughly until combined.

4. Add wet ingredients over the dry ingredients and stir until fully combined. Fold in the cooked sausage.

5. Cook according to your waffle maker's instructions or until steam stops coming out from your waffle maker.

6. Serve with butter and maple syrup.

Sour Cream Waffles

Yields: 4

Ingredients

- 2 large eggs
- 1 cup sour cream
- 1/4 cup butter
- 1 cup buttermilk
- 1 and 1/2 cups all-purpose flour
- 1 teaspoon baking powder
- 1/2 teaspoon salt
- 3/4 teaspoon baking soda

Method

1. Combine sour cream, eggs, buttermilk, and butter.
2. Beat until smooth.
3. In a second bowl, mix baking powder, flour, baking soda, and salt.
4. Add to liquid mixture then stir until fully combined.

5. Cook according to your waffle maker's instructions.

6. Serve and enjoy.

Strawberry Cheesecake French Toast Waffles

Yields: 4

Ingredients

- 2 tbsp. strawberry jam
- 1/4 c. finely chopped strawberries
- 2 eggs
- 1/2 c. milk
- 1/4 tsp. ground nutmeg
- 1 tbsp. sugar
- 1/2 tsp. cinnamon
- 8 slices Challah bread
- Powdered sugar, for dusting
- maple syrup
- 8 tbsp. cream cheese

Method

1. Make cheesecake filling by mixing cream cheese with chopped strawberries and jam until fully combined.

2. Using a shallow bowl, whisk milk, eggs, nutmeg, sugar and cinnamon together.

3. Make sandwiches. Spread cream cheese mixture on a slice of challah then top with another slice. Repeat 4 times.

4. Put the sandwiches in the egg mixture until fully coated.

5. Meanwhile, preheat the waffle iron. When hot, grease with cooking spray. Place a sandwich into the iron and cook until golden brown.

6. Sprinkle with powdered sugar and add maple syrup.

Strawberry Grapefruit Waffles

Yields: 4

Ingredients

For Waffles:

- 1 cup all-purpose flour
- 1 cup milk
- 2 large eggs - beaten
- 2 Tablespoons sugar
- 1 Tablespoon canola oil
- 2 teaspoons baking powder
- 2 teaspoons cinnamon
- 1 teaspoon pink grapefruit zest
- cooking spray

For Toppings:

- 3/4 cup sliced strawberries
- 1/4 cup pink grapefruit juice - strained
- 1/3 cup honey or maple syrup
- additional grapefruit segments - optional
- pats of butter - optional
- powdered sugar – optional

Method

1. Preheat oven to 200 degrees.

2. Using a food processor or a blender, pulse sugar, flour, cinnamon, baking powder, and zest until fully sifted.

3. Add oil, milk, beaten eggs and blend until smooth. Let the batter set for five minutes then cook.

4. Grease the waffle iron with cooking spray and cook waffles according to manufacturer's instructions. Keep waffles warm in the oven.
5. Meanwhile, prepare the topping. Heat grapefruit juice with honey in a small saucepan until warm and fully combined.

6. Top waffles with a bit of butter and strawberry slices or grapefruit slices.

7. Serve and enjoy.

Strawberry Muffles (Waffles from Muffin Batter)

Yields: 3

Ingredients

- 1/2 cup butter
- 3/4 cup sugar
- 2 eggs
- 3 tsp vanilla extract
- 2 cups flour
- 2 tsp baking powder
- 1 cup milk
- 1 1/2 cups sliced fresh strawberries

Method

1. Whisk the butter and sugar until fluffy.

2. Add vanilla extract and the eggs one at a time. Beat thoroughly after each addition of egg.

3. Whisk flour and baking powder together.

4. Gradually add dry ingredients alternately with the milk. Always start and end with an addition of dry ingredients. As a general rule of thumb, add the flour mixture in 3 divisions and the milk in 2.

5. To ensure each muffle gets an even distribution of strawberries, add them to each individual one while cooking. The 1 1/2 cup measurement is just an estimate. You may use less if you prefer.

6. Heat your waffle iron.

7. Pour in your batter and sprinkle several strawberry chunks, then top with the second half of the batter before closing the waffle maker. Cook for about 4-5 minutes until golden brown.

8. Serve with maple syrup.

Strawberry Shortcake Waffles

Yields: 4

Ingredients

FOR THE STRAWBERRY WAFFLES:

- 16 ounces fresh strawberries
- 2 cups Bob's Red Mill Buttermilk Pancake and Waffle Mix
- 4 eggs
- 1/4 cup canola oil
- 1 1/2 cups cold milk

FOR THE MAPLE WHIPPED CREAM:

- 1 cup heavy whipping cream
- 2 tablespoons pure maple syrup

Method

1. Cut the tops of the strawberries and slice. Set aside.

2. In a large mixing bowl, put 2 cups of the pancake and waffle mix.

3. In a second bowl, whisk together the eggs, milk, and oil. Make a hole in the center of dry ingredients then pour in the wet ingredients all at once. Carefully stir until evenly combined. The batter will be a bit lumpy.

4. Cook waffles according to your waffle iron's instructions.

5. Whip the cream using an electric mixer on a medium high speed until it is thickening. Add the maple syrup and continue mixing on high until it is very fluffy and still peaks are forming.

6. Top waffles with strawberries and maple whipped cream.

7. Serve and enjoy.

Super Chocolate Waffles

Yields: 6

Ingredients

- 1 1/2 cups Bisquick baking mix
- 1 cup sugar
- 1/3 cup baking cocoa
- 3/4 cup water
- 2 Tablespoons vegetable oil
- 2 large eggs
- 2/3 cup chocolate chips - optional

Method

1. Combine all ingredients until fully blended. Fold in chocolate chips (if using).

2. Pour batter onto your waffle iron.

3. Bake for about 5 minutes until steaming stops.

4. Plate the waffle and serve with your favorite toppings.

Sweet Potato Waffles

Yields: 12 (4-inch waffles)

Ingredients

- 2 cups sweet potato cubes (1-inch)
- 4 eggs , separated
- 4 tablespoons butter , melted and cooled
- 3/4 cup all-purpose flour
- 3/4 cup whole wheat pastry flour
- 1/4 cup cornmeal
- 1 tablespoon baking powder
- 1 teaspoon ground cinnamon
- 1 teaspoon ground ginger
- 1/4 teaspoon ground coriander
- 1/2 teaspoon sea salt
- 1 cup whole milk
- 1/4 cup granulated sugar

Method

1. Slice sweet potatoes into cubes (1 inch) and set in a sauce pan. Fill it with water, add a pinch of salt, then bring to a boil. Boil for 10 - 12 minutes until soft enough for a fork to get through. Strain and set aside. Mash the potatoes when cool enough so you'll have about 1 1/4 cups mashed sweet potato.

2. Meanwhile, separate eggs and melt butter.

3. Preheat waffle maker. Set oven to 200 degrees F and insert baking sheet to warm.

4. Using a large bowl, mix cornmeal, flours, baking powder, sea salt, and spices.

5. In a medium bowl, combine sweet mashed potato, egg yolks, melted butter, sugar, and milk. Fold wet ingredients into dry ones.

6. Use a beater to beat egg whites to soft peaks and add into batter. Stir until everything is thoroughly mixed.

7. Grease waffle iron with a cooking spray or butter, and then pour the batter onto the waffle maker. Store the cooked ones on baking sheet in warm oven.

8. Serve with Maple syrup.

Tiramisu Waffles

Yields: 4 Waffles (8 Servings)

Ingredients

For Filling

- 1 cup (8oz) mascarpone cheese
- 1/2 cup granulated sugar
- 1/4 teaspoon vanilla extract
- 2 cups heavy cream
- 1 cup brewed lukewarm espresso
- cocoa powder for dusting
- chocolate curls for garnish (optional)

For Waffles

- 6 large eggs (separated)
- 1/8 teaspoon cream of tartar
- 3/4 cup tablespoons granulated sugar (divided)
- 1 1/2 cups all-purpose flour
- 1/2 teaspoon baking powder
- 1 teaspoon vanilla extract
- 1/4 teaspoon salt

Method

1. Preheat your waffle iron.

2. In a bowl of a stand mixer fitted with a whisk attachment, mix cream of tartar and egg whites. Whisk on medium-high speed until foamy.

3. Add 2 tablespoons of granulated sugar then adjust the speed to high.

4. Whip until soft peaks are forming. Move to a clean bowl then set aside.

5. Return bowl to stand mixer and replace the whisk with a paddle attachment.

6. Pour in the remaining 1/4 cup sugar and egg yolks to the bowl. Beat for 1-2 minutes on medium-high speed or until yolks are thick enough and light yellow in color. Add in salt and vanilla.

7. Whisk together baking powder and flour in a small bowl until fully incorporated.

8. Fold into the yolk mixture until stringy (only few streaks of dry ingredients should remain).

9. Fold in the 1/3 of egg whites to lighten. Pour in remaining whites and fold until incorporated. Don't over mix.

10. Pour in the batter to your heated waffle iron and cook until waffles are crisp and golden brown.

11. Preparing the topping: In the bowl of stand mixer with the paddle attachment, mix the sugar, mascarpone cheese, and vanilla.

12. On medium speed, mix until fully incorporated. Pour in the heavy cream and beat until smooth and thickened. If too thick, add another tablespoon of heavy cream as needed.

13. Put brewed espresso in a shallow bowl. Briefly dip each of the waffle's bottom, dipping it no more than 1/3 of the way.

14. Top with a spoonful of the mascarpone mixture, dust with cocoa powder, and sprinkle with chocolate shavings.

15. Serve and enjoy.

Vanilla and Almond Waffles

Yields: 6

Ingredients

- 5 tbs. of melted butter (or 1/3 cup vegetable oil)
- 1 and 1/2 cups self-rising flour
- 1 tbs. of sugar
- 2 large eggs - lightly beaten
- 1 and 1/2 cups milk
- 1 tsp. vanilla flavoring
- 1/2 tsp. almond flavoring

Method

1. Place the sugar and flour into a bowl and stir in the melted butter.

2. Add eggs then stir until smooth. Add the milk gradually to make the waffles nicer and lighter.

3. Once ingredients are fully mixed, add the almond and vanilla then stir again.

4. Cook until golden brown and serve with sauce or fruits.

Veggie Waffles

Yields: 4

Ingredients

- 8 eggs
- 2 cups spinach
- 1 red bell pepper, chopped
- 4 green onions, chopped
- ½ cup parmesan cheese, grated
- ½ cup feta cheese, crumbled
- ½ cup mushrooms, chopped
- 2 tbs. parsley
- ½ cup flour
- 1 tsp baking powder

Method

1. Cook onion and pepper over high heat until soft.

2. Add mushrooms then stir for 2 to 3 minutes.

3. Whip the eggs and stir in baking powder and flour.

4. Stir in parmesan, cooked vegetables, feta, parsley, and spinach.

5. Scoop the mixture into your waffle iron and cook.

6. Serve warm and enjoy.

Waffle Breakfast Tacos

Yields: 4

Ingredients

- 8 frozen waffles
- 8 slices bacon
- 8 large eggs, whisked
- 1 c. shredded white Cheddar
- kosher salt
- Freshly ground black pepper
- Warm maple syrup

Method

1. Preheat oven to 350°. Microwave waffles for 25 seconds until they are pliable but not fully cooked.

2. In a flipped-over muffin tin, place waffles between slots and bake for 5 minutes until they hold their shape.

3. Meanwhile, cook bacon in a large pan over medium heat until crispy. Move to a plate with paper towel to drain. Once cool, break in half. Add half of the fat on the pan.

4. Add eggs to pan and cook, then stir occasionally until scrambled. Add cheese and stir until melted. Remove from heat and add salt and pepper.

5. Line 2 halved bacon strips in each waffle and top with eggs.

6. Drizzle with maple syrup.

Waffle Churros Dippers

Yields: 6 Servings

Ingredients

- 2 c. all-purpose flour
- 1/4 c. plus 2 tbsp. granulated sugar, divided
- 1 1/2 tsp. baking powder
- 1 tsp. baking soda
- Kosher salt
- 2 c. buttermilk
- 3/4 c. (1 1/2 sticks) butter, melted, divided
- 2 large eggs
- 1 tsp. pure vanilla extract
- 1 tbsp. plus 1/2 tsp cinnamon, divided
- 1 c. chocolate chips
- 1/2 c. heavy cream
- Cooking spray

Method

1. Whisk together flour, 2 tablespoons sugar, baking powder, baking soda, and a large pinch of salt in a large bowl. Using another large bowl, whisk buttermilk, 6 tablespoons of butter, eggs, and vanilla together. Gradually add dry ingredients into wet ones and mix with a wooden spoon until fully combined.

2. In a shallow plate or bowl, mix remaining 1/2 cup sugar and 1 tablespoon of cinnamon. Make chocolate ganache by placing chocolate chips and remaining 1 teaspoon of cinnamon in a medium, heat-proof bowl.

3. Heat the heavy cream in a small saucepan over medium-low heat for about 5 minutes until it bubbles. Pour hot cream over chocolate chips. Let it sit for 5 minutes and whisk until smooth.

4. Heat waffle iron and then grease with cooking spray. Pour in the batter.

5. Cook for about 5 minutes until waffles are golden. Repeat with remaining batter.

6. Brush waffles with remaining 6 tablespoons butter and coat with cinnamon-sugar mixture. Serve with ganache.

Waffle Corn Dogs

Yields: 2-4

Ingredients

- 4 hot dogs
- 1 box of corn muffin mix
- 1 large egg
- 1/2 cup sour cream
- 2 tbsp. melted butter
- 1/2 c. shredded Cheddar
- 2 tbsp. chives
- Ketchup and mustard, for dipping

Method

1. Preheat waffle iron.

2. Meanwhile, combine egg, corn muffin mix, and sour cream in a large bowl. Stir until fully combined. Fold in cheddar and chives.

3. Slice hotdog in half lengthwise and in half crosswise. Place a skewer in each piece.

4. Pour half of the batter onto the waffle maker. Place hotdogs on top and then add remaining batter over hot dogs.

5. Close the waffle maker and cook for 4 minutes.

6. Carefully remove the waffle and cut into eighths.

7. Serve and enjoy.

Waffle House

Yields: 4

Ingredients

- 2 cups all-purpose flour
- 1/2 teaspoon baking powder
- 1/4 teaspoon salt
- 1 and 1/2 cups milk
- 8 Tablespoons melted butter
- 4 large eggs - separated
- 1 teaspoon vanilla (optional)

Method

1. In a large bowl, whisk together the flour, egg yolks, melted butter, baking powder, salt, milk and vanilla (if using).

2. Using a second bowl, beat the egg whites to stiff peaks.

3. Fold 1/3 of egg whites into the batter and fold in second third. Once fully incorporated, fold in the remaining egg whites.

4. Cook in a well-greased and hot waffle iron.

5. Serve warm and enjoy.

Waffle Pops

Yields: 20

Ingredients

- 2 c. Bisquick
- 1 1/3 c. milk
- 2 tbsp. vegetable oil
- 1 egg
- Cooking spray, for waffle iron
- popsicle sticks

Method

1. Preheat your waffle iron. Using a large bowl, combine Bisquick, milk, oil, and egg, then whisk together.

2. Use cooking spray to grease the iron. Pour batter into waffle iron and place popsicle sticks on top immediately. Add more batter to cover the popsicle sticks. Cook until the waffles are golden. Remove waffles carefully from waffle maker using a fork.

FOR CONFETTI WAFFLES, CHOCOLATEY BANANA WAFFLES, COOKIES AND CREAM WAFFLE

3. Drizzle white melted chocolate over the waffles and add sprinkles.

4. To make chocolate banana waffles: Drizzle melted peanut butter over the waffles and add banana slices and mini chocolate chips.

5. To make cookies and cream waffles: Drizzle melted chocolate over waffles and sprinkle with crushed Oreos.

Waffle S'mores

Yields: 4

Ingredients

- 1 c. chocolate chips, divided
- 1/3 c. vegetable and canola oil (divided)
- 1/2 c. graham flour (or whole-wheat flour)
- 1/2 c. all-purpose flour
- 1/2 c. graham cracker crumbs
- 1/4 c. cornstarch
- 1 1/2 tsp. of granulated sugar
- 1/2 tsp. baking soda
- 1 tsp. baking powder
- 1/2 tsp. kosher salt
- 1 c. milk
- 1 large egg
- 1 tsp. pure vanilla extract
- Melted butter, for waffle iron
- 1 c. mini marshmallows

Method

1. Preheat the waffle iron to hot setting.

2. Microwave ½ cup of chocolate chips with 1 tsp. of vegetable oil using a microwave-safe bowl for 15-30

seconds intervals until it is melted. Stir until smooth or add oil if the chocolate is not thin enough to drizzle.

3. Using a separate bowl, combine dry ingredients. Pour in egg, milk, and vanilla, then whisk well. Add in remaining oil and chocolate chips. Grease iron with cooking spray or butter then pour your batter onto the waffle maker.

4. Once the waffle is starting to take a golden brown color, add ¼ cup of marshmallows on top of it. Put another waffle on top, making a sandwich. Close the waffle maker for about 30 seconds to melt the mallows.

5. Serve waffles on a plate and drizzle with melted chocolate.

Waffogato (Waffles w/ Vanilla Ice Cream and Coffee)

Yields: 2

Ingredients

- Prepared waffle batter
- Melted butter, for dunking
- 1/4 c. sugar
- 2 tbsp. ground cinnamon
- Vanilla ice cream, for serving
- Hot coffee, for serving

Method

1. Prepare classic cooked waffles.

2. Allow your waffles to cool then prepare the sugar dredging station.

3. In a shallow bowl, pour your melted butter and dunk the waffles in the bowl while making sure both sides are properly coated. On another plate, mix sugar and cinnamon then dunk the waffle in the cinnamon sugar mix.

4. Top your waffle with 1-2 scoops of Vanilla ice cream (or other flavor of your choice) and then drizzle hot coffee over your ice cream. Serve and enjoy.

Whole Grain Blueberry Waffles

Yields: 8

Ingredients

- 1 cup frozen and thawed blueberries
- 1 and 1/2 cups reduced-fat milk
- 3/4 cup all-purpose flour
- 1/2 cup quick-cooking oats
- 1/2 cup whole wheat flour
- 1 large egg - lightly beaten
- 2 tbsp. vegetable oil
- 3 teaspoons baking powder
- 1/4 teaspoon salt

Method

1. Preheat your waffle iron.

2. Sift together oats, flours, salt, and baking powder in a large bowl.

3. Using a second bowl, stir milk, egg, and vegetable together.

4. Add wet ingredients into dry ingredients and stir until large lumps disappear. Don't over mix.

5. Fold in blueberries.

6. Cook waffles in a well-greased and hot iron. Serve and enjoy.

Whole Grain Waffles

Yields: 4

Ingredients

- 1 cup all-purpose flour
- 3/4 cup whole wheat pastry flour
- 1/4 cup quick or old-fashioned oats
- 1/4 cup flax seed meal
- 1/4 cup wheat germ
- 4 teaspoons baking powder
- 2 Tablespoon sugar
- 1/4 teaspoon salt
- 2 large eggs - beaten
- 1 and 3/4 cups milk
- 1/4 cup applesauce
- 1/4 cup vegetable or canola oil
- 1 teaspoon vanilla extract

Method

1. Mix all dry ingredients in a large bowl (oats, flours, wheat germ, flax meal, sugar, baking powder, and salt).

2. In a second bowl, combine the milk, eggs, applesauce, vanilla, and oil.

3. Pour in wet ingredients to dry ingredients and mix until smooth.

4. Heat the waffle iron and cook until crisp and golden brown.

5. Serve with maple syrup.

Whole Wheat Banana Waffles

Yields: 5

Ingredients

- 1 1/3 cup whole wheat flour
- 1 cup skim milk/buttermilk
- 1/3 cup egg whites
- 1/4 cup non-fat plain yogurt
- 2 teaspoons baking powder
- 3/4 teaspoon salt
- 1/2 medium banana (diced)

Method

1. Beat the egg whites for a few minutes then add yogurt, milk, flour, and salt. Beat until everything is fully blended.

2. Add the baking powder and beat continuously.

3. Pour the batter onto your heated waffle iron and add the diced banana on top before closing the iron.

4. Cook according to your waffle maker's instructions.

Whole Wheat Waffles

Yields: 6

Ingredients

- 1 1/3 cup whole wheat flour
- 1 cup milk
- 2 large eggs (separated)
- 4 Tablespoons melted shortening
- 2 Tablespoons sugar
- 2 teaspoons baking powder
- 3/4 teaspoon salt

Method

1. Vigorously beat the egg yolks in a bowl then add milk and shortening.

2. Using a second bowl, mix the sugar, flour, and salt. Add to the first mixture and beat until smooth.

3. Beat egg whites until stiff peaks form.

4. Fold into the batter.

5. Lightly sift the baking powder over the mixture and quickly fold in.

6. Cook in a lightly-greased waffle iron.

7. Serve warm and enjoy.

Whole Wheat Yeast Waffles

Yields: 12

Ingredients

- 1 1/2 cup Whole Wheat Pastry Flour
- 2 1/4 teaspoons (1 package) yeast (active dry or instant)
- 1 1/2 teaspoons salt
- 2 tablespoons unsalted butter, melted
- 1/3 cup oil
- 3 tablespoon brown sugar
- 3 cups milk (I used 1%)
- 4 eggs
- 2 1/4 cup all purpose flour
- 1 teaspoon vanilla extract

Method

1. Using a large mixing bowl, combine flours, yeast, and salt.

2. In a medium saucepan or large microwave-safe bowl, mix melted butter, oil, brown sugar and milk. Heat to 120º to 130º

3. Pour liquid ingredients to dry ingredients and blend on low speed until combine.

4. Add vanilla and eggs. Beat for 2 to 3 minutes on medium speed

5. Cover the bowl. Refrigerate batter several hours or overnight.

Wonuts (Waffle Donuts)

Yields: 4-6

Ingredients

- 1 c. all-purpose flour
- 1 tsp. baking powder
- 1/4 tsp. baking soda
- 1/2 tsp. kosher salt
- 1 Egg, lightly beaten
- 3/4 c. sugar
- 1/4 c. milk
- 1/4 c. sour cream
- 2 tsp. vanilla extract
- 1/2 c. melted chocolate chips
- Rainbow sprinkles
- Cooking spray

Method

1. Preheat waffle maker.

2. Mix flour, salt, baking powder, and baking soda in a medium bowl. Using a separate small bowl, whisk milk, sugar, sour cream and vanilla together until fully combined. Add wet mixture over dry ingredients and stir until combined.

144

3. When the waffle iron is hot, use cooking spray to grease. Add about 1/4 cup of batter into the iron and cook until the Wonut is golden. Put on a cooling rack as you cook the rest.

4. Add melted chocolate on the center of each Wonut and top with the rainbow sprinkles. Serve and enjoy.

Yeast Waffles

Yields: 6

Ingredients

- 1/2 cup warm water (110 degrees ideal)
- 1 quarter-ounce package of active dry yeast
- 2 cups milk
- 3 cups sifted all-purpose flour
- 1/2 cup melted butter -
- 2 Tablespoons sugar
- 1 teaspoon salt
- 3/4 teaspoon vanilla
- 1/2 teaspoon cinnamon (optional)
- 2 large eggs - lightly beaten
- 1/2 teaspoon baking soda

Method

1. In a small bowl, dissolve the yeast and let it stand for 10 minutes until creamy.

2. In a sauce pan, warm the milk over medium to low heat until it's the same temperature as the warm water.

3. In a large bowl, combine the warm milk, yeast mixture, melted butter, flour, salt, sugar, cinnamon,

and vanilla. Beat until batter is smooth.

4. Cover the mixture and leave at room temperature overnight for at least 6 hours (no more than 16).

5. The next morning, preheat your waffle iron.

6. Add the beaten eggs and baking soda to the batter and beat until fully combined.

7. Cook according to your waffle maker's instructions.

Yeast Waffles (Quick)

Yields: 5

Ingredients

- 1 3/4 cups milk
- 8 tablespoons (1 stick) cold unsalted butter
- 2 cups all-purpose flour
- 1 tablespoon sugar
- 1 1/2 teaspoon instant or rapid-rise yeast
- 1 teaspoon salt
- 2 large eggs
- 1 teaspoon vanilla extract

Method

1. In a small sauce pan, heat the butter and milk over medium heat. When about half of the butter has melted, turn off the heat and continue stirring until the remaining butter melts. Allow it to cool for a few minutes.

2. In a separate bowl, whisk together the sugar, flour, salt, and yeast, until fully combined. Set aside.

3. Whisk together the eggs and vanilla in a small bowl then set aside.

4. Carefully pour the warm milk over the flour mixture and whisk until fully incorporated. Stir in the egg mixture until it starts thickening.

5. Cover with a plastic wrap and let it rise for about 60 minutes (you should see bubbles on the surface of the batter).

6. Stir the batter and cook according to your waffle maker's instructions.

7. Serve warm and enjoy.

Conclusion

I want to thank you once again for purchasing this book.

Waffles are wonderful in every way, shape, and form – and as a bonus, they are extremely easy to make. If you are anything like me, you would have to agree that there is nothing quite like waking up to the smell of crispy and scrumptious waffles in the morning.

Or for lunch and dinner for that matter.

The various recipes in this book will suit absolutely any occasion that you can think of, offering you an abundance of opportunities to explore, experiment, and of course eat, a whole world of waffles that you hadn't even imagined.

So again, what are you waiting for?

Thank you, and please enjoy!

Other Books by Grizzly Publishing

"Jamaican Cookbook: Traditional Jamaican Recipes Made Easy"
https://www.amazon.com/dp/B07B68KL8D

"Brazilian Instant Pot Cookbook: Delicious Pressure Cooked Meals Made Fast and Easy"
https://www.amazon.com/dp/B078XBYP89

"Norwegian Cookbook: Traditional Scandinavian Recipes Made Easy"
https://www.amazon.com/dp/B079M2W223

"Casserole Cookbook: Delicious Casserole Recipes From Around The World"

https://www.amazon.com/dp/B07B6GV61Q

Made in the USA
Columbia, SC
06 November 2023

25596219R00095